PAMPHLETS ON AMERICAN WRITERS · NUMBER 25

UNIVERSITY OF MINNESOTA

Washington Irving

BY LEWIS LEARY

UNIVERSITY OF MINNESOTA PRESS · MINNEAPOLIS

Distributed to high schools in the United States by
McGraw-Hill Book Company, Inc.
New York   Chicago   Corte Madera, Calif.   Dallas

PUBLISHED IN GREAT BRITAIN, INDIA, AND PAKISTAN BY THE OXFORD
UNIVERSITY PRESS, LONDON, BOMBAY, AND KARACHI, AND IN
CANADA BY THOMAS ALLEN, LTD., TORONTO

WASHINGTON IRVING

↲ *Washington Irving*

F ew writers have successfully stretched a small talent farther than Washington Irving. He was an alert, ingenuous man who liked to be liked, and who tried to write what other people expected of him. His success was at once the measure of his own placid adaptability and of assurance among most of his contemporaries that literary excursions should be pleasantly trivial, skipping over surfaces without disturbing deeper matters of trade or politics, the opening of the West or decisions on what democracy should be. People who spoke their minds sharply, like Philip Freneau or Fenimore Cooper, held Irving in great scorn, but almost everyone else admired him. He was comfortable to have around, for he seldom raised his voice, and he flattered his countrymen's assumption that they were, in truth, gentlefolk who could sip appreciatively on Old World culture at the same time that they built new traditions of strength and hardihood.

Irving spoke out at a time when his country needed someone like him. No longer was quizzical Ben Franklin, sage but uncouth, to represent the best in native accomplishment. People had already begun to talk of him as a despoiler of polite language and cultivated taste. His influence made for penny-pinching vulgarities, so that even poetry from the New World often spoke of commerce as a be-all and end-all. Many Englishmen of discrimination seemed to agree with Dr. Samuel Johnson that there was something degenerate about most Americans. Few were surprised at the scorn in Sydney Smith's tone as he asked in 1820, "Who reads an American book?"

When Washington Irving's *The Sketch Book* appeared at just

that time, as if to provide by its popularity an answer to the question, literature of the United States gave first promise of eventual maturity. It had lived through a difficult, war-torn childhood, and for years was to struggle through an awkward adolescence. Clothed often in castoff garments, pampered, and praised for the wrong things, nurtured more often in parlor or library than in its spacious backyard, it nonetheless grew, its voice wavering and cracking, until finally, by the time of Irving's death in 1859, it had learned to communicate with authenticity and persuasion. During the years between, when Emerson and Hawthorne spoke most clearly, when Thoreau was thought strange and Poe shocking, when Melville and Whitman wrote of matters beyond the experience of many men, then Irving was more famous and respected than any of these, the dean indeed of American letters, envied by Cooper, admired by Longfellow, whose deft extensions of Irving's moods made him seem his logical successor.

Neither Irving nor Longfellow is esteemed so highly now, but neither is forgotten. The latter's songs still occasionally gladden or gently lull, and Irving, at the very least, has presented his country with the inestimable gift of two characters and a name. Either Rip Van Winkle or Ichabod Crane would be recognized at once if he walked down almost any American street. Their adventures have become as much a part of native lore as Captain Smith's rescue by Pocahontas, Tom Sawyer's slick whitewashing deal, or Paul Bunyan's gargantuan strength and appetite. In much the same sense, the word *knickerbocker* has become, through Irving's use of it, more than a designation for a baggy Dutch garment: it describes a period in the history of native culture, and an attitude toward literature and life; it appears today almost one hundred times in the Manhattan directory, to identify, among others, a fashionable corps of cadets, a brewery, a bookshop, a professional basketball team, and a manufacturer of plastics.

But Irving's reputation during his lifetime rested on greatly more than this, and a candid revaluation of his writing today suggests more also. He had two effective voices. As Diedrich Knickerbocker, he spoke of native themes, with crusty vigor — almost everything of Irving's which is most affectionately remembered is put in the words of that unpretentious and sometimes impolite old gentleman. As Geoffrey Crayon, he was decorous and superbly polished, beloved as an ambassador of good will between the New World and the Old, who lifted the literary embargo on both sides by disproving "the old notion that it is impossible for an *American to write decent English*." Praised by Scott and Byron and Moore, Irving became a solid, cheerful, adaptable symbol of what a proper man of letters might be. As much as Franklin, he studied the way toward success.

Like Franklin also, he was the last child born in a large family, but without forebears deeply rooted in colonial America, as Franklin's had been. Irving's dour Presbyterian father had come to New York from Scotland only two decades before the birth of his youngest son on April 3, 1783, just as the Revolution drew to a close. In spite of wartime troubles, William Irving had prospered, and was assisted now by his oldest son and namesake, already at seventeen active in the family wine, sugar, hardware, and auctioneering business. The next son, Peter, was two years away from entrance to Columbia College, where he would receive preliminary training toward a medical degree which he was never to use. Seven-year-old Ebenezer was musical, but already promised to be the steadiest of them all, destined for a career in trade. John Treat, five years older than the youngest Irving, would also attend Columbia, to prepare in law. The three sisters married early and moved away, but wrote affectionate letters home which testify to close-knit family ties.

As the youngest, Washington Irving seems to have been a

7

spoiled child, precocious, moody, and sensitive, and subject to alarming bronchial attacks. "When I was very young," he remembered, "I had an impossible flow of spirits that went beyond my strength. Every thing was fairy land to me." From the age of six to fifteen, he was doomed, he said, "to be mewed up the lifelong day in that purgatory of boyhood, a schoolroom." Thereafter, instead of entering college, he read haphazardly in whatever books came to hand, and explored nooks and crannies of little New York: "I knew every spot," he said, "where a murder or robbery had been committed, or a ghost seen." More often, he wandered about the countryside, seeking health, it was explained, in the open air. Sometimes he adventured along the banks of the Hudson River, even above Spuyten Duyvil and Yonkers, through Dutch villages to Tarrytown, where his brother William's wife's family, the Pauldings, lived, "adding greatly to my stock of knowledge," he said, by noting rural habits and customs, and conversing with country people. Passing through Sleepy Hollow to the Pocantico Hills, he could look across the river to the legend-haunted headlands of the lower Catskills.

Between excursions, after 1799, he read law intermittently, finally with Josiah Ogden Hoffman, who had two attractive daughters. During the summer of 1803, he made a long journey with the Hoffmans, by boat and oxcart into Canada, squiring the girls, playing his flute, reciting Shakespeare, and filling notebooks with impressions of moonlight over the Hudson, of trading with Dutch farmers for milk and cheese, of squalid frontier lodgings and overland travel through deep-rutted forest roads, alert for whatever was comic or picturesque or appealed to sentiment.

For he had already, at nineteen, become known to contemporaries as a person of "extraordinary . . . literary accomplishments," deserving of the best "admiration and esteem." When the previous autumn his brother Peter had become editor of the new

Morning Chronicle in New York, Irving contributed a series of nine sportive letters, from November 15, 1802, to April 23, 1803, over the signature of "Jonathan Oldstyle, Gent." They played with grave pleasantry over the state of manners, dress, and marriage in New York, but with greatest enthusiasm over the state of the theater. The jingoistic drama of the time — brave American sailors in love and at war — was lampooned; actors were caricatured, and musicians who with "solemn and important phizes" produced discordant noise; the managers were chided for not keeping the playhouse clean or the playgoers quiet; and critics were taunted as "pests of society," who attended performances only to "lounge away an idle hour."

Jonathan Oldstyle was so merry and vulgar an old gentleman that a more sedate Irving was later to be ashamed of him, but he spoke zestfully, and colloquially well. He disliked candle-grease dripping on his jacket from the theater chandeliers, and he became tired of dodging apple cores thrown by rowdies in the gallery. Jonathan discreetly ogled the belles who smiled flirtatiously from the boxes, their charms set off to most alluring advantage — here an arched look, there a simper, everywhere bewitching languish. He was sorry that spyglasses were no longer used to observe them more closely. And the critics — "ha! ha!" — how foolish and subversive: "they reduce feelings to a state of miserable refinement, and destroy entirely all the enjoyments in which our coarser sentiments delighted."

Much of what Irving would do best is foreshadowed in these juvenile essays: the physical caricature, which Dickens would admire and imitate — the dapper Frenchman, the persnickety spinster, the talkative old gentleman, the suave but foolish gallant, and the honest countryman "gazing in gaping wonder"; the pose of nostalgia — "Nothing is more intolerable . . . than innovation"; the rich delight in describing food and feasting — "the hissing of

9

frying pans, winding the savory steams of roast or boiled." Most predictive, however, are the style and manner: the tailored sentences, well buttoned with adjectives; the jocular good humor, vulgar sometimes, but seldom ribald; the quip and the laugh and the quick retreat before feelings are deeply hurt; and through all the sense that Irving liked the people at whom he flicked his whimsically bantering wit — "that quiet, shrewd, good-humored sense of the ridiculous" which contemporaries recognized as setting Irving apart "from every other writer in our language," but which never of itself was enough to ensure him place as a major writer.

Perhaps because they did prick republican pretensions and looked shrewdly down their nose on native manners, the Oldstyle essays established young Irving as a kind of social arbiter for young America. Charles Brockden Brown, fresh from minor triumphs as a novelist, invited him to contribute to his *Philadelphia Literary Magazine*. Joseph Dennie, who conducted the *Port Folio* as "Oliver Oldschool," recognized and applauded the literary kinship implied by his choice of pseudonym. During the spring of 1804, Irving probably contributed to Peter's short-lived, astringent *Corrector*, and he continued his precocious career as a wit among men and a favorite with the ladies. His health, however, did not withstand even such pleasantly diversified pastimes, and he was packed off in May for a recuperative voyage to Europe.

The traveling did him good, in health and spirit. He made new friends and learned new manners, and filled notebook after notebook with careful records of what he saw and did, whether reverently viewing castles and cathedrals or in hairbrained escapades with his companions. He endured pirate attacks, excursions through bandit-infested hills, rough rides, bad lodgings, and poor food, picking up smatterings of French, Spanish, and Italian, reading volume after volume of travel adventures written by other men, and flirting with exotic women, now with novices in a convent, at another time with country damsels at a wayside tavern. Even the Italians, he wrote his father, "stared at us in surprise and called us the *wild Americans.*"

In Rome, he met Madame de Staël, and was astonished that any woman could talk so much and so well. In Genoa, he met Washington Allston, the American artist, who almost persuaded him to remain in Italy to study painting. In Paris, he visited the tailors and the theater, and was thrilled to be accosted on the street by handsome, predatory young women. In London, he saw Mrs. Siddons at Covent Garden — in fact, he saw every play he could, and wrote home about them enthusiastically in detail. By the end of twenty-three months, however, Irving admitted that "one gets tired of travelling, even in the gay and polished countries of Europe. Curiosity cannot be kept ever on the stretch; like the sensual appetites, it in time becomes sated." He was happy therefore "once more [to] return to my friends, and sink again into tranquil domestic life."

Back in New York, he entered a scattered round of activities, reserving just enough time for the study of law to allow him to pass his bar examinations late in 1806. He helped Peter translate a travel book from the French; he contributed to the *Literary Picture Gallery*, a periodical dedicated to activities of visitors at Ballston Spa; he wrote occasional verse, including doggerel lines for the opening of the New Park Theater. Perhaps it was of himself that he spoke when later he allowed a character to confess: "I had too much genius for study . . . so I fell into bad company, and took to bad habits. Do not mistake me. I mean that I fell into the company of village literati, and village blues, and took to writing village poetry. It was quite the fashion in the village to be literary."

They were gay blades, those "lads of Kilkenny" — Peter and Gouverneur Kemble, Henry Brevoort, Henry Ogden, James Kirke

Paulding, the Irving brothers, Peter and Washington and some-times William — the "worthies" who met for literary powwows at Dyde's tavern, and for "blackguard suppers" at a porterhouse on Nassau Street: "sad dogs" indeed, fond of conscientious drinking and good fun. Among their favorite haunts was the old Kemble mansion on the Passaic River, about a mile above Newark, which they renamed Cockloft Hall; they transferred to it much of the fictitious adventure set forth in *Salmagundi*, a periodical which, when it appeared in twenty numbers irregularly from January 24, 1807, to January 25, 1808, became the talk and wonder of the town. "If we moralize," they promised, "it shall be but seldom, and on all occasions, we shall be more solicitous to make our readers laugh than cry; for we are laughing philosophers, and truly of the opinion that wisdom, true wisdom, is a plump, jolly dame, who sits in her arm-chair, laughs right merrily at the farce of life — and takes the world as it comes."

Who wrote it was soon suspected — the Irvings, Washington and William and perhaps Peter, and William's brother-in-law, James Kirke Paulding; but who wrote what has never been determined, so mixed and various but unified in temper was the matter set forth as "the whim-whams and opinions of Launcelot Langstaff, Esq., and others." Usually "Anthony Evergreen, Gent.," com-mented on fashionable society; "William Wizard, Esq.," handled theatrical and literary critcism; "Pindar Cockloft" contributed verse; and Launcelot Langstaff, as proprietor, roamed at will over all subjects. "In hoc est hoax, cum quiz et jokesez. Et smokem, toas-tem, roastem folksez, Fee, faw fum," they asserted on the title page in a cryptic motto, which was obligingly translated as "With baked and broiled, stew'd and toasted, and fried, boil'd, smok'd and roasted, we treat the town."

"As everybody knows, or ought to know," the first issue began, "what a SALMAGUND is, we shall spare ourselves the trouble of an explanation; besides we despise trouble as we do everything low and mean, and hold the man who would incur it unnecessarily as an object worthy of our highest pity and contempt." Most people, however, have been tempted to look up the word, to discover that it describes an appetizer made of chopped meat (raw), pickled herring, and onions, liberally seasoned with olive oil, vinegar, and cayenne pepper — excellent, some find, with cocktails or beer. No less savory were the elements compounded in *Salmagundi*, expertly mixed to encourage "genuine honest American tastes" rather than fashionable "French slops and fricasseed sentiment." For the convenience of readers, it was printed "on hot-pressed vellum paper, as that is held in highest estimation for buckling up young ladies' hair," in size just right for fitting "old ladies' pockets and young ladies' work bags."

The ladies came in for a great share of attention as the young men from Cockloft Hall labored to "instruct the young, reform the old, correct the town, and castigate the age." The ladies of New York were "the fairest, the finest, the most accomplished, the most ineffable things that walk, creep, crawl, swim, float, or vegetate in any or all of the four elements," but how alarmingly they dressed — in flesh-colored stockings and off-the-shoulder gowns: *"nudity* being all the rage." Actors and critics received sharp flicks, and fashionable upstarts like "Ding Dong," Ichabod Fungus," and "Dick Paddle." Open war was declared against local folly and stupidity, especially in the letters of "Mustapha Rub-a-Dub Khan," written unashamedly in imitation of Oliver Goldsmith's "Citizen of the World" essays. Boorish English travelers and foppish French dancing masters were laughingly derided; even so popular a favorite as Thomas Moore, recently a visitor to America, was reproved for having "hopp'd and skipp'd our country o'er,"

> . . . sipped our tea and lived on sops,
> Revel'd on syllabubs and slops,

And when his brain, of cob-web fine,
Was fuddled with five drops of wine,
Would all his puny loves rehearse,
And many a maid debauch — in verse.

All was good humor, laughingly sustained, even when the satire turned political, like that directed against Thomas Jefferson, his embargo, his red riding breeches, and his scientific interest in "impaling butterflies and pickling tadpoles." More bitter invective was reserved for literary rivals, like Thomas Green Fessenden, an outlander, recently from New England, who in his *Weekly Spectator* dared criticize *Salmagundi* as a frothy imitation of Addison and Steele. "From one end of the town to another," he complained, "all is nonsense and 'Salmagund.' America has never produced great literature — her products have been scrub oaks, at best. We should, then, encourage every native sapling; but when, like *Salmagundi*, it turns out to be a *bramble*, and pricks and scratches everything within its reach, we naturally ask, why it encumbereth the ground."

Quarreling which turned bitter was not to the taste of the lads from Cockloft Hall; it was certainly not to Irving's, who for all his wit, was shy, more fond of conciliation than argument. *Salmagundi* was intended only as "pleasant morning or after-dinner reading, never taking too much of a gentleman's time from his business or pleasures." It was calculated for the mood of New York, "where the people — heaven help them — are the most irregular, crazy-headed, quick-silver, eccentric, whim-whamsical set of mortals that were ever jumbled together." Though frivolous and derivative *Salmagundi* was expertly done. If it were possible to know what parts of it Washington Irving wrote, they would probably be recognized as almost as good as anything he ever did.

Not only did *Salmagundi* hurt feelings; it was also not profitable — or so the young men claimed when they suspended publication after a year. Footloose again, Irving enjoyed his friends in Washington, Philadelphia, and New York, where he played lightly in chaste drawing-room flirtations with lovely ladies in the highest society and, with gentlemanly disdain, in politics. At Richmond, he helped Josiah Hoffman defend Aaron Burr in his trial for treason. He wrote occasional verse and squibs, and perhaps contributed political commentary to the newspapers, composing what was expected of him — usually at someone else's request. But ever since the decease of *Salmagundi*, he had been casually at work on a book of his own.

He and Peter had started it together, as a parody of a guidebook to New York, but when Peter was called abroad as manager of the family business in Europe, Washington Irving completed it alone — in grief, it has been said, and sadness. For on April 26, 1809 — a date which he never forgot — young Matilda Hoffman died, she on whom Washington Irving's errant attentions had at length settled. His heartbreak was so great, and finally so well known, that it has become a commonplace to suppose that Irving remained all his life a bachelor because of loyalty to Matilda Hoffman's memory: "her image was continually with me, and I dreamt of her incessantly."

But, however sorrowful the months through which Irving brought it to completion, *A History of New York from the Beginning of the World to the End of the Dutch Dynasty*, which appeared in December 1809, remains his first unified and his most joyous book. He wished it thought to have been written by a strange, inquisitive little gentleman named Diedrich Knickerbocker, who had disappeared, leaving behind him the manuscript of this "only authentic history of the times that hath been or ever will be published." Fact was jumbled with fiction, some dates were wrong, some footnotes spurious, but it was a gay, mirth-filled book. The "unutterable ponderings of Walter the Doubter, the disas-

15

trous projects of William the Testy, and the chivalric achievements of Peter the Headstrong" had New York in an uproar; when they reached England, they made Walter Scott's sides, he said, "absolutely sore with laughter." But many people of Dutch descent resented it: horsewhipping was spoken of, and ostracism. Emerson was later to disapprove of Knickerbocker's "deplorable Dutch wit," and Whitman of his "shallow burlesque." More feelings were hurt than Irving had intended.

Yet Knickerbocker's *History* continues lightheartedly to beguile readers of later generations, who enjoy its lovely comic pose — its "Münchausen vein of exaggeration run mad" — without being bothered by attempts to identify every victim of Irving's satire. John Adams may be recognized, and perhaps James Madison; no one will miss Thomas Jefferson, who is ridiculed for his "cocked hat and corduroy small clothes," and his eccentric, democratic manners. What lives, however, are not these things, any more than what lives in *Gulliver's Travels* are the political allusions which scholars discover there. Byron prized Knickerbocker's *History* for its copious style; Dickens is said to have worn out his copy with eager reading; and Coleridge to have stayed up all one night to finish his. Not every modern reader will respond as heartily, but none will find Irving more consistently pleasant to be with than in this boisterous book which he completed at the age of twenty-six.

His laughter is directed at historians, explorers, plump Dutch matrons, and robust Connecticut girls, at Yankee skinflints and parsons, cock-fighting Virginians, the cozy pleasures of bundling and overeating (in luscious detail). As a resident of "the beloved isle of Manna-hata," Knickerbocker looked with suspicion on New Englanders as "pumpkin-eating, molasses-daubing, shingle-splitting, cider-watering, horse-jockeying, notion-peddling" creatures. Colonists to the south "lived on hoe-cakes and bacon, drank mint julips and brandy toddy," and amused themselves with "slave-driving, tavern-haunting, Sabbath-breaking, and mulatto-breeding." Frontiersmen were "a gigantic, gunpowder race of men . . . exceedingly expert at boxing, biting, gouging, tar and feathering" — "half man," they were, "half horse, half alligator."

The extravagance, mock gravity, and massive irreverence which was to characterize American humor from Sam Slick through Mark Twain to Faulkner are anticipated as Irving describes a sunbeam falling on the giant red nose of Antony the Trumpeter as he leaned over the side of a ship plying the Hudson, then bouncing off, "hissing hot," into the water "to kill a mighty sturgeon that was sporting beside the vessel." Wouter van Twiller, "exactly five feet six inches in height and six feet five inches in circumference," was a man of such extraordinary wisdom that he avoided disturbances of the world by closing his eyes for hours at a time, his active intelligence producing all the while "certain guttural sounds, which his admirers declared were merely the noise of conflict made by his contending doubts and opinions."

Irving's weapon was less often the rapier than what Stanley Williams has described as a "true Dutch blunderbuss, shooting off in all directions." More often than not, the humor is broad, sometimes mirthfully vulgar, as when brave Peter Stuyvesant, harassed in a duel, falls backward "on his seat of honor," to land kerplunk on a meadow "cushion, softer than velvet, which providence or Minerva, or St. Nicholas, or some kindly cow, had benevolently prepared for his reception." No wonder his countrymen were scandalized when Irving compared a Dutch ship to a maiden from New York: "both full in the bows, with a pair of enormous cat-heads, a copper bottom, and a most prodigious poop!"

Legend is created and local legend is utilized as Irving shaped from whatever came to his quick-moving hands a mirage of tradition, through which characters moved in quixotic grandeur, their noble pretensions made absurd, though no less noble, because of the provincial background against which they suffered inevitable, comic defeat. His reading was ransacked for archetypal patterns against which native heroes could be measured: at the Battle of Fort Christina, "immortal deities, who whilom had seen service at the 'affair' of Troy — now mounted their feather-bed clouds and sailed over the plain," until "victory in the likeness of a gigantic ox-fly, sat perched upon the cocked hat of the gallant Stuyvesant." How ludicrously small the deeds of warriors in this New World "when contrasted with the semi-mythic grandeur with which we have clothed them, as we look backward from the crowned result, to fancy a cause as majestic as our conception of the effect." With these words, James Russell Lowell was perhaps the first to recognize that Irving, as much as Cooper, though with lighter touch, produced a "homespun and plebeian mythos" — in Fielding's terms a "comic epic" — in which gallant protagonists tested ideals of the Old World against the frontier requirements of the New.

There was theme and scheme behind the "coarse caricature" of Knickerbocker's *History*. The *Monthly Anthology* of Boston greeted it as a book "certainly the wittiest our press has ever produced." In Philadelphia, the *Port Folio* praised its "drollery and quaintness," its "copious and natural style." Neither recognized it, as did the *Athenaeum* in London a few years later, as "an honest and manly attempt to found an American literature. Those who read it must have exclaimed involuntarily, 'Yes, this is the work which was wanted. The umbilical cord is severed. America is indeed independent.'" For not even Irving quite knew what he had done; when he revised the *History* a few years later, he cleansed it of much colloquial coarseness, and of caricature which might wound, apparently so intent on being liked that he failed to realize that he had written the first American book capable of outliving the man who made it. Only Franklin's *Autobiography* claims precedence, for reasons quite different.

Irving's book is more irresponsible, more fun, and more literary. Source hunters have searched libraries to discover every influence on it, and none has done the job to another's satisfaction. Sterne and Fielding were certainly on Irving's mind, imitated or parodied; Swift, Cervantes, Shakespeare, Rabelais, the King James Bible, Aesop, Homer, Thomas Malory, and Thomas Paine are all present, in allusion or idiom; Arthurian legend, Greek myth, and the ponderous supposings of Cotton Mather's *Magnalia Christi Americana* jostle one another in exuberant disarray. Historians have derided or defended his adaptation of fact to fancy, sometimes locating in some half-forgotten volume in Latin, French, or Dutch the phrase or incident which Irving wove into a fabric not quite like any other.

Knickerbocker's *History* brought some profit (two thousand dollars) and more renown: "I was noticed, caressed, and for a time elated by the popularity I had gained"; but "this career of gayety and notoriety soon palled on me. I seemed to drift without aim or object." A second edition was called for in 1812, another in 1819; it was translated to French and German, and adapted for the stage. But it marked the end of one phase, the most carefree and lavish, of Irving's literary career. Not again would he write with such abandon; seldom would he write so spontaneously well. Grief or circumspection, or the enervating deceleration of spirits called growing up, sobered Irving.

In 1810, he became a partner in the family hardware business, but was apparently expected to devote little time to its routine affairs. Instead, he went to Washington as a lobbyist against restrictions in trade, and there he spent many hours in seeing the town with Paulding, and attending official balls, where he became a favorite of Washington's favorite hostess, Dolly Madison. Back in New York, he prepared a brief biographical introduction for an American edition of the poems of Thomas Campbell, declaring that in "an age when we are overwhelmed by an abundance of eccentric poetry, it is really cheering and consolatory to behold a writer . . . studiously aiming to please."

Irving's consistent demand of literature was that it should please, and more by familiarity than strangeness. As editor for two years beginning in January 1813 of the *Analectic Magazine*, he warned readers against Wordsworth's "new and corrupt fashion of writing," preferring instead the comfortable rhythms of Scott and Byron, the "warm sensibilities and lively fancies" of Thomas Moore. Friends complimented him for having "sacrificed his elegant leisure" thus to contribute to the literary advancement of his country, but Irving was bored and restless. He grumbled about the routine of editorial work and the quality of materials he found to print: "I really stagger under the trash." Paulding contributed an occasional short story, and joined the editor in a series of sketches of naval heroes. Irving himself conducted a column of "literary intelligence," wrote undiscriminating reviews, and published a handful of sketches, among them the "Traits of Indian Character" and "Philip of Pokanoket," which he would later resurrect to fill out the pages of *The Sketch Book*.

Finally, in 1815, "weary of everything and myself," he set out again for Europe, determined "to break off . . . from idle habits and idle associates and fashionable dissipation." There he hoped to "pursue a plan I had some time contemplated, of studying for a while, and then travelling about the country for the purpose of observing the manners and characters of various parts of it, with a view to writing a work which, if I have any acquaintance with my talents, will be far more . . . reputable than anything I have yet written."

In England, he visited with relatives and old friends, explored romantic byways of London, called on Campbell and Moore, breakfasted with Samuel Rogers, went on literary pilgrimages to

Kenilworth, Warwick, and Stratford, but most reverently to Abbotsford, where Scott welcomed him cordially. He studied German so that he could read legends which Scott admired. He wrote some tales of his own and assiduously noted impressions, in words or deftly sketched drawings, of each new scene. He helped whenever necessary with the family business, filling in as he could for Peter who was increasingly unwell. When, toward the end of 1817, the commercial enterprises of the Irving brothers faced bankruptcy, William, now in Congress, tried to get government positions for the two brothers stranded in England, and did manage an appointment for Washington, who turned it down, because, he said, "My talents are purely literary. . . . I do not wish to undertake any situation that must involve me in routine duties."

Faced now, in his mid-thirties, for the first time with the necessity of depending on himself for support, Irving took stock of his literary wares: he reworked Knickerbocker's *History* for new publication, thumbed through his journals for usable materials, and reminisced with friends about incidents which might be turned to account. He feared, however, that his mind had lost "much of its cheerfulness and some of its activity." When early in March 1819 he sent home a packet of manuscript, he apologized, "I have attempted no lofty theme, nor sought to look wise and learned. I have preferred addressing myself to the feeling and fancy of the reader rather than to his judgment. My writing, therefore, may seem light and trifling."

But with the appearance in New York two months later of the first number of *The Sketch Book of Geoffrey Crayon, Gent.*, Irving's reputation rose at once to a level from which nothing he had done before or would do again would budge it. A pamphlet of ninety-three pages, in gray-brown paper covers, it contained five sketches, the first four skillfully done but commonplace, and the fifth, "Rip Van Winkle," the slender, indestructible peg on which much of his fame has ever since been hung. Six more numbers were issued in New York, irregularly over the next sixteen months, until September 1820, each greeted with applause and admiration.

When parts of *The Sketch Book* began to appear, without permission or profit, in English periodicals, Irving early in 1820 arranged for a London edition of the whole, first done at his own expense; but soon — thanks to assistance from Scott, to whom in gratitude (or perhaps to set right those readers who supposed Scott had written the pseudonymous work) the edition was dedicated — it was issued by John Murray in two attractive volumes which sold prodigiously well in printing after printing. Of its thirty-two essays and sketches, twenty-six were about England, six of them descriptive of London scenes and five celebrating old-time Christmas festivities at an English country house; two were asides — "The Voyage" and "The Spectre Bridegroom"; and four were on American themes, two of these the Indian sketches from the *Analectic* which had not appeared in the periodical publication of *The Sketch Book* in New York.

Scott thought the book delightful, not so "exclusively American" as Knickerbocker's *History* and *Salmagundi*; William Godwin admitted that he hardly knew an Englishman who could write so well. Few contemporary readers seemed to agree with Wordsworth that *The Sketch Book*, "though a work of talent, is disfigured by an abundance of affectations"; more thought Irving, as Southey did, "a remarkably agreeable writer," with touch light enough "to conciliate any reader." These pleasantly diverting samples from Geoffrey Crayon's portfolio were shaded with humor and delicately colored with sentiment, not studied "with the eye of a philosopher; but rather with the sauntering gaze with which humble lovers of the picturesque stroll from one shop window of a print shop to another; caught sometimes by the distortions of caricature, and sometimes by the loveliness of landscape."

Familiarity added to the charm of the sketches. Scott's influence was plain throughout, his fastidious archaizing and untidy eloquence, later so distasteful to Mark Twain. Strokes learned from Addison were clearly discernible, and moods borrowed from Goldsmith's *The Deserted Village*, Thomson's *The Seasons*, Cowper's *The Task*, and Crabbe's somber rustic vignettes. So soft and adroitly accommodating was his touch that Irving was constantly compared to someone else, as if he had not manner or substance of his own — to Sir Thomas Browne, Fielding, Smollett, Sterne (never Swift, though sometimes Defoe), but especially to the ruminative and moralizing essayists of the eighteenth century. As an artist, he seemed copyist rather than creator: his literary offspring, said one unkind commentator, "resemble a family of sickly, but pretty children, — tall, feeble, and delicately slender, with white hair and white eyes, — dressed in jaconet muslin, trimmed with pink ribbon."

In England, his "eye dwelt with delight on neat cottages, with their trim shrubberies and green grass plots," on "the mouldering abbey overgrown with ivy, with the taper spire of a village church rising from the brow of a neighboring hill." His landscapes were stylized in the manner of the Flemish colorists whom he admired. Broad, traditionally evocative strokes pictured "vast lawns that extend like sheets of vivid green, and here and there clumps of gigantic trees, heaping up rich piles of foliage: the solemn pomp of groves and woodland glades, with deer trooping in silent herds across them; the hare bounding away to the covert; or the pheasant, suddenly bursting upon the wing; the brook, taught to wind in natural meanderings, or expand into a glassy lake: the sequestered pool, reflecting the quivering trees, with the yellow leaf sleeping on its bosom, the trout roaming fearlessly about its limpid waters; while some rustic temple or sylvan statue grown

23

green and dank with age, gives an air of classic sanctity to the seclusion."

More important than the scene was the mood which it called forth, of serenity — "classic sanctity," wherein each once free-flowing brook is *taught* to wind in what are made to seem, but which are not, "natural meanderings"; or made to "expand into a glassy lake" which calmly reflects the lethargic quiescence which the scene suggests. Geoffrey Crayon's still waters have little depth; the irrepressible bright flow of language with which Diedrich Knickerbocher spoke of old New York had been taught to conform to London manners. Though he admired, Irving said, the elegance and strength, robustness, manliness, and simplicity of the English gentleman, these were not traits which he easily transferred to his laboriously correct, embellished prose. He was not, it can be said, to the manor born.

Even the portraiture which as Geoffrey Crayon he now contrived was less vibrant, and the humor more timidly mannered. A line or two, whimsically suggestive because stylized, was often enough to represent a person — "the little swarthy Frenchman," for example, "with a dry weazen face, and large whiskers." Sometimes the portrait is briefly elaborated, like that of the angler in "broad-skirted fustian coat perplexed with half a hundred pockets; a pair of stout shoes, and leathern gaiters; a basket slung one side for fish; a patent landing net, and a score of other inconveniences." What people looked like was more important than what they were. Even in detailed "characters," like that of "John Bull," Irving assiduously balanced every blemish with some appealing trait.

Careful now that feelings should not be hurt, his comic pose was altered. "Wit, after all," he explained, "is a mighty tart, pungent ingredient, and much too acid for some stomachs; but honest good-humor is the oil and wine of a merry meeting." In a world so roiled, who was he to venture a disturbing idea? "If, however, I can by some lucky chance, rub out one wrinkle from the brow of care, or beguile the heavy heart of one moment of sorrow . . . I shall not have written in vain."

Exactly what happened to Irving's comic sense has not been adequately explained. Perhaps it was caution — once burned, twice shy; or perhaps it was maturity, which may be the same thing, or a desire to be liked, which is not. Always dependent on crutches made of other men's literary manner, Irving once had agility enough sometimes to dance a little jig of his own, using the rubber-tipped supports to beat out a muffled accompanying rhythm; or, like some temporarily crippled athlete, had swung from them a breath-taking two steps at a time up some hazardous stairway of ridicule. Now he learned to use them more sedately, careful that his own feet, once bruised by criticism, should touch the ground no more often than necessary, but with his gait so well adjusted to other people's that they hardly noticed his using crutches at all. Some even remarked that he got on very well without them when he adventured in American themes.

But even when he spoke as Diedrich Knickerbocker, Irving was accused of plagiarism. The plot of "Rip Van Winkle" was shamelessly stolen. Passages from the old German tale of "Peter Klaus" have been placed side by side with passages from Irving's narrative, to reveal imitation so blatant that much of Rip's unhappy experience seems little more than direct translation. But such bookish detective work may miss much of Irving's intention. "I wish in every thing I do," he once declared, "to write in such a manner that my productions may have something more than mere interest in narrative to recommend them, which is very evanescent; something, if I may use the phrase, of classic merit, i.e. depending on style . . . which gives a production some chance for duration beyond the whim and fashion of the day."

Something more than style, however, has kept Rip Van Winkle alive, on stage, on screen, and in the hearts of his country-men. He has become their "muse of memory," Hart Crane once said, their "guardian angel of a trip to the past," and he remains their conscience, accusing and amusing at the same time. As Irving gave local habitation to a myth, perhaps as old as any which has beguiled the mind of man — that of Epimenides, Endymion, Sleeping Beauty, and the seven sleepers of Ephesus — he added such other familiar elements of popular lore as the thunder of the gods, birds of ill-omen, a magic potion, man's canine best compan-ion, and dwarfs who are spectral spirits, transporting Valhalla and the Brocken to the Catskills, where Rip still triumphantly postures as the man-boy American (Huck Finn and Anse Bund-ren) who never grows up, the New World innocent who yearns to return to prelapsarian freedom from work and responsibility, to retire like Franklin at forty and fly a kite. "A child playing with children," he has been called, "a kid with a dog."

Before Fenimore Cooper or Mark Twain, Henry James, Sinclair Lewis, or William Faulkner, Irving created — it may be thought inadvertently — a symbol of the mythic American, presenting, as Philip Young has pointed out, "a near-perfect image of the way a large part of the world looks at us: likeable enough, up to a point and at times, but essentially immature, self-centered, careless and above all — and perhaps dangerously — innocent. Even more point-edly Rip is a stereotype of the American male as seen from abroad, or in some jaundiced quarters at home: he is perfectly the jolly overgrown child, abysmally ignorant of his own wife and the whole world of adult men — perpetually 'one of the boys' " — a Lazarus come back from the dead, as if to warn his countrymen, and yet a comic figure, in spite of the tragedy of a life slept away. His son is like him, and his grandson is another Rip.

Irving himself was surely not consciously so devious a contriver — it is the critics who have found him out. When in "The Legend of Sleepy Hollow," he adapted parts of Bürger's *Der Wilde Jäger*, and perhaps Robert Burns's "Tam O'Shanter" also, Irving admitted the tale "a random thing, suggested by scenes and stories about Tarrytown"; its borrowed plot was "a mere whimsical band to connect descriptions of scenery, customs, manners." Yet in creating Brom Bones and Ichabod Crane, and the contest between them, he has been recognized as "the first important American author to put to literary use the comic mythology and popular traditions of American character which, by the early nineteenth century, had proliferated widely in oral tradition," demonstrating that "Dutch rowdies of the upper Hudson Valley were frontiersmen of the same stamp as the Ohio riverboatmen and Missouri trappers."

The Dutch of "The Legend of Sleepy Hollow" are indeed different from the chuckle-headed, indolent, pipe-smoking, stoop-sitting Dutch burghers of Irving's earlier writings. Brom is a frontier braggart, burly and roistering, "a Catskill Mike Fink, a ring-tailed roarer from Kinderhook." He is the sturdy backwoodsman who tricks the tenderfoot, acting out for the first time in our literature, says Daniel G. Hoffman, a theme which "has proliferated ever since: in Davy Crockett, in Mark Twain, in thousands of dime novels and popular magazines in which the yokel gets the best of the city slicker." Ichabod, a jack of many trades — schoolmaster, singing teacher, farmer, and eventually a successful lawyer — is rightly designated as Irving's Connecticut Yankee, a comic and less spectacular ancestor of Mark Twain's mechanic, a more optimistic witness to the common man's fate than Melville's Israel Potter. Obtrusively pious, this psalm-singing son of New England, naive and superstitious, but shrewdly ambitious, his head filled with daydreams of quick wealth through union with the "blooming Katrina" and setting out with her toward riches of the frontier, "for Kentucky, Tennessee, or the Lord knows where" — bloodless

Ichabod is father to many confident, untrained, blundering, successful native heroes, and is the American cousin certainly of Dickens' Uriah Heep.

Almost all of Irving's better remembered tales thus celebrate victory for the practical man, defeat for the dreamer — as if they were modest or masochistic sardonic parables of his own career. Men like Brom, who understand or defy superstition and know that visions are illusory, come out well. Fancy must be replaced by common sense as one grows older: tales of goblins, or even of high adventure and romance, are for children or childish men. What an ironic twinkle must have accompanied Irving's postscript notification to readers that even an ungainly visionary like Ichabod Crane turned out well, when he left daydreaming, as Irving had not, and turned to law.

As Diedrich Knickerbocker rather than Geoffrey Crayon speaks, the technique of broadly sketched caricature is managed with surer touch: readers do not forget Ichabod Crane astride his boney nag, the short stirrups bringing "his knees nearly up to the pommel of the saddle; his sharp elbows stuck out like grasshoppers'; he carried his whip perpendicularly in his hand, like a sceptre, and, as his horse jogged on, the motion of his arms was not unlike the flapping of a pair of wings." Dickens seldom displayed more gustatory fervor than Irving when he described "the ample charms of a genuine Dutch country tea-table" — the "doughty doughnut, the tenderer oly koek, and the crisp and crumbling cruller," the abundance of pies and meats and poultry, and "delectable dishes of preserved plums, and peaches, and pears, and quinces . . . all mingled higgledy-piggledy."

Not Hawthorne or Balzac or Frank Harris at his descriptive best could better have presented Mynheer Van Tassel's spacious farmhouse, over which "a great elm tree spread its broad branches . . . at the foot of which bubbled up a spring of the softest and sweetest water in a little well formed of a barrel; and then stole sparkling away through the grass to a neighboring brook that bubbled along among alders and dwarf willows." Beneath its low-projecting eaves were "flails, harness, various utensils of husbandry, and nets for fishing"; inside the house were "rows of resplendent pewter, ranged on a long dresser."

"In one corner stood a huge bag of wool ready to be spun; in another a quantity of linsey-woolsey just from the loom; ears of Indian corn, and strings of dried apples and peaches, hung in gay festoons along the walls, mingled with the gaud of red peppers . . . claw-footed chairs and dark mahogany tables shone like mirrors; and irons with their accompanying shovel and tongs, glistened from their covert of asparagus tops; mock-oranges and conch-shells decorated the mantel-piece; strings of various colored birds' eggs were suspended above it; a great ostrich egg was hung from the centre of the room, and a corner cupboard, knowingly left open, displayed immense treasures of old silver and well-mended china."

Without Rip Van Winkle and Ichabod Crane, and Diedrich Knickerbocker to tell their stories, *The Sketch Book* would still be a pleasantly diverting, but an undistinguished, collection. The Christmas sketches, the observations on country customs, the descriptions of Westminster Abbey, Stratford-on-Avon, and Boar's Head Tavern contain painstakingly colored vignettes of people and of venerable scenes. "The Art of Bookmaking" is a good-natured spoof of the manner in which Irving himself culled from writers of the past. His remarks on "The Mutability of Literature" are engaging rephrasings of melancholy certainties about there being no end to the making of books, or to mute, inglorious authors who are fated to write unknown. In his mild rebuke to "English Writers on America," Irving comes perilously close to expressing ideas which might offend.

From this time on, the spirit of Geoffrey Crayon almost completely took charge, and manner became increasingly more important than matter. "I consider the story," Irving repeated a few years later, "merely as a frame on which to spread my materials. It is the play of thought, and sentiment, and language; the weaving in and out of characters lightly, yet expressively delineated; the familiar and faithful presentation of scenes of common life; and the half-concealed vein of humor that is often playing through the whole; — these are what I aim at." But his aim was uncertain: when friends advised him to try longer fiction, he objected that anyone could write a novel — "the mere interest of story . . . carries the reader through pages and pages of careless writing, and the author may be dull for half a volume at a time, if he has some striking scene at the end of it." In composition such as he preferred, the "author must be continuously piquant; woe to him if he makes an awkward sentence or writes a stupid page."

Yet like Poe, who also disputed the effectiveness of longer fiction, Irving did not turn aside from the novel until he had tried to write one and discovered that he did not do it well. Though *Bracebridge Hall, or, The Humorists* was offered in 1822 as a "medley" of fifty-one sketches centered about an English country house, it is in fact a novel-*manqué*, faintly derisive and winsomely derivative. Squire Bracebridge may have been modeled, as Irving once suggested, on Walter Scott, but General Hardbottle, Lady Lillycraft, the village antiquary, and the faithful family retainers come direct from memories of characters better drawn by Goldsmith and Sterne. Ghost stories, bits of village gossip, essays on falconry, fortunetelling, and love-charms are strung almost haphazardly on a slender thread of romance, which ends with the wedding of Fair Julia, a shy, exemplary English girl, adroitly a caricature of heroines of sentimental fiction.

But most endearing of the sketches in *Bracebridge Hall* are not the village tales which form its substance but the fillers, the stories told as evening pastime at the ancient country house. Suspense is artfully created in "The Stout Gentleman," and exotic charm in "The Student of Salmanaca," but not as successfully as in "Dolph Heyliger" and "The Storm Ship," both re-creations of Hudson River lore drawn "from the MSS. of the late Diedrich Knickerbocker." Once again, however, these native tales were exceptions, for the New World offered little of appeal comparable to that of Europe. In America, Irving explained, all was "new and progressive, and pointed to the future rather than to the past"; there all "works of man gave no ideas but of young existence," without historical associations such as Irving found in England, where he wandered happily, "a grown-up child," he said, "delighted with every object."

"Never need an American look beyond his own country for the sublime and beautiful of natural scenery," he had said in *The Sketch Book*. "But Europe held forth charms of storied and poetical association. There were to be seen the masterpieces of art, the refinements of highly-cultivated society, the quaint peculiarities of ancient and local custom. My native country was full of youthful promise: Europe was rich in the accumulated treasures of age. Her very ruins told the history of times gone by, and every mouldering stone was a chronicle. I longed to wander over the scenes of renowned achievement — to tread, as it were, in the footsteps of antiquity, — to loiter about the ruined castle, — to meditate on the falling tower, — to escape, in short, from the commonplace realities of the present, and lose myself among the shadowy grandeurs of the past." Irving meant what Cooper, Hawthorne, Henry James, and Van Wyck Brooks later were to mean when they spoke of what America lacked which Europe had — the sustaining sense of history, and a decorum bred by tradition; but, perhaps because he said it first, he did not say it as clearly as they.

31

He searched through Europe now for more tales to retell, in a series of new collections — a German sketch book, an Italian, a Spanish, a French. "There are," he observed, "such quantities of these legendary and romantic tales now littering the press," needing only, as he had said, the polish of style to improve them. So he set out for the Continent in 1823, filling more notebooks with observations on quaint ceremonials, boar hunts, old castles, and bright national costumes — anything calculated to delight the eye or excite the imagination. But he worked by fits and starts, for he was not well, and he was forty: "My sunny days of youth are over." In Dresden, he puttered over translations, entertained himself and his friends with amateur theatricals, and courted young Emily Foster, who thought him too old. In Paris, where French editions of his writings made him seem a man of importance, he collaborated with John Howard Payne on plays, none of which was successful; he considered a book on Napoleon, worked over a series of American tales, planned an edition of English classics, and a play based on the life of Shakespeare.

After two dilatory years, hounded by his publisher for new materials but unable to collect enough of any one kind for a new book, in the summer of 1824 Irving threw together what he had into *Tales of a Traveller* — a mélange of German stories, tales of Italian banditti, an abortive novelette, and more American sketches "found among the papers of the late Diedrich Knickerbocker." Though containing some of the liveliest writing which Irving had done since leaving America, and presenting in "The Devil and Tom Walker" his third-best native tale, the collection was not well received. We have heard these stories all before, said *Blackwood's*: the characters are corpses in clumsy new clothing. Irving was called "indisputably feeble, unoriginal and timorous; a mere adjective of a man, who had neither vigor nor courage to stand alone."

If it were to bring such dubious returns, further travel seemed a wearisome prospect. Irving considered writing a life of Byron, of Cervantes — tempted now to suspect that he was by nature a biographer, which he was; and he worked long hours over a projected American sketch book — and then either destroyed or lost the manuscript. His talent, he thought, was blighted, the romance of life past. When early in 1826, he was invited to join the staff of the American Legation at Madrid, he welcomed the opportunity to settle in one place. He vowed again to work assiduously, and for three years he did.

Irving was wanted in Spain, not as a diplomat, but as a writer, to translate Don Martín de Navarette's recently published collection of documents relating to Columbus. The work was congenial and appealingly sedentary: Irving rummaged with such zeal through old libraries for collateral materials that when Longfellow called on him that spring, he was astounded at the older man's energy — up at six, at his desk through the day. Incidents from Navarette's book were elaborated with bits and pieces from other chronicles, and the whole was polished until it shone attractively as a straightforward narrative of exotic color and maritime adventure. But by the time the four volumes of *The Life and Voyages of Christopher Columbus* were issued in the summer of 1828, Irving was excitedly involved with another book, more surely his own, which he hoped might recapture, though with circumspection, something of the ironic tone of Knickerbocker's *History*.

Assuming the pseudonym of Fray Antonio Agapida, a zealot monk, who distorted history, "marring the chivalry of the camp by the bigotry of the cloister," Irving presented the *Chronicle of the Conquest of Granada* in 1829 as "something of an experiment": a book made "out of old chronicles, embellished, as I am able, by the imagination, and adapted to the romantic taste of the day — something that was . . . between a history and a romance." William H. Prescott and Francis Parkman were to do this kind of thing better; but Irving did it first, mingling "romance and satire with grave historical details" as he told the story of Boabdil, last Moorish king of Granada, a dashing man in love or battle. But irony filters only dimly through these corpse-strewn fields lighted by flashes of sunlight on the "exterminating scimitar"; as halls resound with shrieks and fountains run red with blood, the spirit of old romance so illuminates each of its one hundred brief and chiseled chapters that Prescott declared Irving's *Granada* was permeated with such "dramatic brilliancy denied to sober history" that it "superseded all further necessity for poetry."

The *Voyages and Discoveries of the Companions of Columbus*, in 1831, was another modified translation, expertly done and well received. Meanwhile, however, Irving had been traveling again — through the "rugged valleys and long, naked, sweeping plains" of southern Spain, where he was captivated by the "proud, hardy, frugal, and abstemious" country people, and by the stories they told and the songs they sang; and he had settled in the old Moorish castle of the Alhambra. Through most of the spring and into the summer of 1829, Irving threw all his energies into a Spanish sketch book which, when published in 1832 as *The Alhambra*, would revive his reputation as "the first English prose-writer of the day," an artist with a true and tender eye for the unusual or picturesque, with feeling for scene at once precise and emotionally expansive.

The luxuriant southern sun, quiet countryside, and remains of oriental splendor in the ancient Moorish stronghold seemed "too beautiful to be real": "As I loiter through these oriental chambers, and hear the murmur of fountains and the song of the nightingale; as I inhale the odor of the rose and feel the influence of the balmy climate, I am almost tempted to fancy myself in the paradise of Mahomet." He admired the refinement of those Moorish "princes of a departed and almost forgotten race, who reigned in elegance and splendor in Andalusia, when Europe was in complete barbarism," their achievements in art and education, their benevolent administration of justice. How splendid was this past, when "lovers of the gay sciences resorted to Cordova and Granada, to imbibe the poetry and music of the east; and the steel-clad warriors of the north hastened thither, to accomplish themselves in the grateful exercises and courteous usages of chivalry."

Irving's love of ancient lore, his feeling for scenery, his sentiment for people as simple, tranquilly suffering, but well-meaning and utimately good, seldom had been better exercised than in *The Alhambra*, which for generations has vied with *The Sketch Book* as the most popular of his works, anticipating Flaubert, Pierre Loti, Stevenson, and Lafcadio Hearn in luxuriant sensuality. If all seems surface polish and prettiness; if dark areas are lighted with too soft a glow; if "manly defiance of hardships, and contempt of effeminate indulgence" again seem traits inappropriately honored by a person of Irving's haphazard sensibility, *The Alhambra* nonetheless does present him at his burnished best and at his wayward worst. The story of Peregil, the water carrier, in the "Legend of the Moor's Legacy" combines pathos and humor with narrative skill, to produce another minor masterwork; the rest of *The Alhambra* blends to a deliquescent glow which is remembered as pleasant long after details are forgotten.

Fame now completely engulfed Washington Irving, celebrated in the press of two continents as a purveyor of culture from the Old World to the New, and as the good-natured explainer of American idiosyncrasies to Europe: his writings went through half a hundred editions, and were translated into a dozen languages. On leaving the Alhambra in the later summer of 1829, Irving returned to London as secretary to the American Legation there. The next year, he received a medal from the Royal Society of Literature, and he edited Bryant's *Poems* for publication in England, changing some of the words to make them conform to British taste. The year after that, he was awarded an honorary doctorate at Oxford. Then, following a final tour to Stratford and Kenilworth, he set out for home, something he had contemplated doing every year, he said, for the past seventeen years.

On May 23, 1832, he once again saw "the bright city" of his birth. New York provided him a hero's welcome, with a ceremonious dinner at the City Hotel, where the halls "rang with bravos, handkerchiefs were waved on every side, three cheers given again and again," as Irving, tears in his eyes, announced that he was home to stay, and that, above all, he loved America: "It was the home of the heart." He visited Saratoga Springs and Niagara Falls, and as the result of a chance meeting with a commissioner to the Indians, made a four-month trip into the Pawnee country of the Southwest, recording excitedly in his journal each new scene of picturesque interest.

Back in New York that winter, among friends now as sedate but not nearly so famous as he had become, plaudits continued to be showered on him. He declined nomination to Congress, as he would later decline nomination by Tammany Hall as candidate for mayor of New York, and appointment by President Van Buren as secretary of the navy. Instead he engaged himself to John Jacob Astor — for a tremendous sum, it was rumored — for the purpose of going over that self-made millionaire's papers, to make a book from them about the opening of the West and the fur trade. In 1836, he moved to an old Dutch farmhouse below Tarrytown, which he first named "Wolfert's Roost," and then "Sunnyside," a "little, old-fashioned, stone mansion, all made up of gabled ends, as full of angles and corners as an old cocked hat."

The Crayon Miscellany had appeared in 1835, most of it taken up with the lively *A Tour on the Prairies,* but pieced out with memorials of Abbotsford and Newstead Abbey to make it of book length. Often reprinted as another "minor American classic," a book to be placed beside Parkman's *The Oregon Trail* or even Mark Twain's *Roughing It,* Irving's *Tour* has gone through more than thirty editions in English and twenty in translation. Because, in Irving's words, it is "a simple narrative of everyday occurrence," with "no wonders to describe, nor any moving accidents by flood or field to narrate," it represents to readers with little patience for whimsey or sentimental humor the crown of Irving's work. It offers them a rugged Irving, with trousers tucked inside his boots, gun in hand, fording streams, sprawled (elegantly perhaps) beside a campfire.

Unlike *Astoria*, in 1836 ("Not even WASHINGTON IRVING," said one reviewer, "can beat furs into eloquence"), or *Adventures of Captain Bonneville*, in 1837, both of them, like the Spanish histories, suavely adapted from other men's accounts, *A Tour on the Prairies* recounted Irving's own discovery of the frontier West. He noted the "gypsy fondness" of Creek Indians for brilliant color and gay decorations, the proud independence of the Pawnee ("sons of Ishmael, their hand is against everyone"), and the fine, Roman features of the Osages; their manly independence reminded him, almost twenty years before Thoreau expressed the same thought in *Walden,* that "we in society are slaves, not so much to others as to ourselves; our superfluities are the chains that bind us." Some forecast of the tone of Lambert Strether, who also learned in his middle years that he had never really lived, creeps into Irving's voice when, over fifty, he admits, "We send our youths abroad to grow luxurious and effeminate in Europe; it appears to me that a previous tour of the prairies would be more likely to produce that manliness, and self-dependence, most in unison with our political institutions."

37

But, though he spoke of trappers as a "rabble rout of non-descript beings" who hover like bats "about the frontiers between civilized and savage life"; though he described his half-breed guide as "one of the worthless brood engendered and brought up among the missions," who "fancied himself highly connected, his sister being concubine to an opulent white trader"; and though he sometimes caught in dialogue the clipped colloquialism of the native woodsman ("Next to my rifle, I'd as leave lend you my wife"), Irving's old manner of piquant phrase and romantic extension crept often into his record of these frontier experiences, especially when he retold at second hand the stories of hunting and Indian warfare, tall tales recounted by trappers, and Indian legends which had "a wild romantic interest heard from the lips of half-savage narrators." His brief chapter on "The Bee Hunt" may deserve comparison with William Bartram's account of Florida alligators, or Thoreau's description of the battle of the ants; but the brief vignette of forest rangers in bivouac, in a "wild bandit" or "Robin Hood" atmosphere, is another set piece of the kind at which Geoffrey Crayon had always excelled — an assemblage of particularized notations, memoranda in an artist's field book: "Some were cooking at large fires made at the feet of trees; some were stretching and dressing deer skins; some were shooting at a mark, and some were lying about in the grass. Venison jerked and hung on frames, was drying over embers in one place; in another lay carcasses recently brought in by the hunters. Stacks of rifles were leaning against the trunks of trees, and saddles, bridles, and powder-horns hanging above them, while the horses were grazing here and there among the thickets."

But pictures like this, carefully drawn from observation, seldom appeared in what Irving now considered his more important work. He grumbled about imitators who climbed toward fame with sketch books of their own, none quite done in his painstaking manner, not even Longfellow's *Outre-Mer* in 1834, which spoke of Europe and its legends. John Pendleton Kennedy's *Swallow Barn* in 1832 seemed simply a Virginian adaptation of *Bracebridge Hall*, not to speak of Cooper's *The Pioneers* nine years earlier, which told of an old family mansion on the frontier, and James Hall's *Legends of the West*, which skimmed most of the good stories from that region. Nathaniel Parker Willis had done a *Pencillings by the Way*, and Augustus Longstreet a boisterous *Georgia Scenes*, both in 1835. Irving had no heart for continuing in competition with any of these, or with the younger men like Hawthorne, who admired him, or Poe, who thought him pallid, or Emerson, whose remarks on self-reliance and throwing off shackles of the past may have seemed a rebuke.

Instead, at Sunnyside from 1837 to 1842, Irving rummaged through old notebooks for materials capable of being reworked, "writing away *like fury*," said Longfellow, on "remnants — odds and ends, — about Sleepy Hollow, and Granada. What a pity!" Another Spanish book was on his mind, a history of the conquest of Mexico, but he gave that up when he learned that Prescott was engaged with the subject, turning instead to an even more "American" theme — a life of George Washington which, like the *Columbus*, might examine roots of New World tradition, providing indisputable evidence that strength and resolution and solid sense and gallantry had been from their beginning characteristic of the best of his countrymen.

To the *Knickerbocker Magazine* in New York he contributed sketches and tales — "a hodgepodge of his experiences from the age of eighteen to fifty-eight," which were to be collected in *Wolfert's Roost* in 1855 and in the posthumous volume of *Spanish Papers*. "Mount-Joy: or Some Passages Out of the Life of a Castle-Builder" made good-natured fun of Transcendentalists "who render many of our young men verbose and declamatory, and

39

prone to mistake aberrations of their fancy for inspirations of divine philosophy," and both "The Great Mississippi Bubble" and "The Early Adventures of Ralph Ringwood" are sprawling narratives of frontier life which look tentatively toward the lustier ironic realism of Mark Twain.

These better things were few, however, and not greatly different from other contributions by younger Americans who now vaunted their devotion to native scene and theme; but the Irving stamp was on them, certifying their authenticity by a style which shaped whatever subject to his familiar moods. He reworked his biography of Campbell and the sketch of Goldsmith which he had first done in Paris fifteen years before. Few books written during these decorous years were more popularly applauded than his sentimental *Biography and Poetical Remains of the Late Margaret Miller Davidson* of 1841, in which Irving spoke tenderly about the yearnings and aspiring verse of a tremulous, tubercular girl who had died at the age of sixteen, only a year younger than Matilda Hoffman had been when she died.

Early in 1842, Irving accepted appointment as minister plenipotentiary to the court of Spain, a position which came to him as the result of an apparent political about-face which had Fenimore Cooper — just then caged about by legal controversies with Whig opponents — growling in disgust. During the next few years, briefly in England and then in Madrid, Irving played a modestly important role as a diplomat, lending his prestige and suave good humor to negotiations over Cuba, the Oregon boundary dispute, and defense of his country's attitude in the Mexican War, "though I regret to say my endeavors have occasionally been counteracted by the derangement of my health." By the late summer of 1846, he was happy to be back once more at Sunnyside, which he would not leave for long again.

"In the early part of my literary career," he remembered, "I used to think I would take warning by the fate of writers who kept on writing until they 'wrote themselves down,' and that I would retire while still in the freshness of my powers — but . . . circumstances have obliged me to change my plan, and I am likely to write until the pen drops from my hand." Day after day at Sunnyside, he tinkered over old writings and projected new. In 1849 he arranged with George P. Putnam for a revised edition of his works, which would finally grow from fifteen to twenty-one, to twenty-seven volumes. *Mahomet and His Successors*, over which he had been worrying for almost a quarter of a century, appeared in 1850, to be followed by the miscellaneous *Wolfert's Roost* five years later, a book which it pleased him to find praised in the London *Spectator* as filled with "as much elegance of diction, as graceful a description of natural scenery, as grotesque an earnestness in diablerie, and as quiet but telling a satiric humor, as when Geoffrey Crayon came before the English world, nearly forty years ago."

Meant as praise, these words describe much of Irving's literary fortune, and foretell the inevitable decline of his reputation. For forty years there had been no change. This man of limpid style was without a subject, except as he could find it ready-made, available for transforming to language adroitly adapted to popular taste. Adventures as revealed in old tales or old documents, nostalgic recollection of bygone scenes, and the fallible, lovable, admirable characteristics of people — these were the themes which brought Geoffrey Crayon fame. Diedrich Knickerbocker could do better, and did, slipping into each miscellaneous volume a tale or two which gives it body, usually through the creation of characters indelibly drawn.

For it was finally people who interested Washington Irving most — whimsical people, droll manifestations of popular whimwhams; people who drifted as he had drifted, from one project to another, searching the key to success; or successful people, the

41

heroes of whom Carlyle had written, and the representative men of whom Emerson spoke. Irving's life had been checkered with plans for biographies never completed, of Byron, Napoleon, Cervantes. The lives of English poets which he had supplied as hackwork introductions spurred his ambition to do something larger. The popular success of the little book about Margaret Davidson made him think he could do even better.

He did do greatly better with *Oliver Goldsmith*, one of the most appealing literary biographies of the first half of the nineteenth century. It was "a labor of love," said Irving, "a tribute of gratitude to the memory of an author whose writings were the delight of my childhood, and have been a source of enjoyment to me throughout life." Done in three versions, first in Paris in 1825 as an introduction to the Goldsmith volume in Galignani's series of English Classics, expanded in 1840 as *The Life of Oliver Goldsmith, with Selections from His Writings* in Harper's Family Library, it was published in final form as *Oliver Goldsmith: A Biography* by Putnam in 1849. Though much of its material is drawn from Sir James Prior's and John Forster's more complete studies, Irving's *Oliver Goldsmith* outlives either, partly because, as Hazlitt recognized, its author "binds up his own portrait with Goldsmith's."

Irving admired "the artless benevolence" of Goldsmith, the "whimsical, yet amiable views of human life and nature; the unforced humor, blending so happily with good feeling and good sense, and singularly dashed at times with a pleasing melancholy" —all characteristics which readers for so many years had been accustomed to associate with Irving's own writing. Each, it has been said, looks "at human nature from the same generous point of view, with the same kindly sympathies, and the same tolerant philosophy"; each has "the same quick perception of the ludicrous, and the same tender simplicity in the pathetic"; in each runs "the same quiet vein of humor, and the same cheerful spirit of hopefulness." Irving defended his own literary intentions when he praised Goldsmith's writings because they "sweeten our tempers, and harmonize our thoughts; they put us in a good humor with the world, and in so doing they make us happier and better men."

Veneration and a sense of responsibility got in the way, however, as Irving devoted his final, failing energies to the *Life of George Washington*, the first volume of which appeared in 1855. Planned for three volumes, the work dragged on, filled with fact and anecdote and with massive descriptions of military events; too seldom graced even with vestiges of Irving's former easy prose, it moves by fits and starts, as if pushing desperately toward completion. "The shadows of departed years," he confided to a friend, "are gathering over me." But, he said, "I must get through with the work which I have cut out for myself. I must weave my web, and then die."

Scarcely six months after seeing the fifth and last volume of the *Life of George Washington* through the press, on November 28, 1859, Washington Irving died. At his funeral "thousands from far and near silently looked for the last time on his genial face, and mourned his loss as that of a personal friend and national benefactor." His grave in Sleepy Hollow Cemetery is still carefully attended, and flowers are placed in Christ Episcopal Church in Tarrytown each year on the anniversary of his death. The old house at Sunnyside has been restored, and schoolchildren make pilgrimages there to see the room where Washington Irving wrote.

For his reputation does live on, not perhaps among somber critics, for Irving was not in their sense a dedicated or committed person. But for those who accept in literature what they find there, and who are experienced enough not to expect too much, refreshing discoveries are to be made in reviewing his writings. It will not do to think of Irving as a complicated man. With quick eye, ready tongue, and alert recognition of absurdities, he sits quietly at both ends of the American literary spectrum — an expatriate seeking reverently in Europe for sources of culture, but, like James and Eliot and Pound, most effective in realizing American characters enmeshed in American ideals; and at the same time a native myth-maker who wove indigenous lore into comic tales which become fables. His country's first, but not her best, romantic historian; an early, but unsatisfying, impressionistic biographer; an exotic local colorist before Flaubert popularized the term; a mildly boisterous, thigh-slapping, sidesplitting rural humorist, a comic realist before Thackeray, a caricaturist before Dickens — Irving was tentatively all of these. He writes better than anyone who has written of him, in praise or condemnation; and he shares with each critic the handicap of having little of final importance to write about.

⊿ Selected Bibliography

Principal Writings of Washington Irving

IRVING'S collected writings have appeared in more than forty editions, one not greatly different from another; most often available is the Author's Uniform Revised Edition: *The Works of Washington Irving* (New York: G. P. Putnam's Sons, 1860–61), in 21 volumes. See Stanley T. Williams and Mary E. Edge, *A Bibliography of the Writings of Washington Irving* (New York: Oxford University Press, 1936).

"Letters of Jonathan Oldstyle, Gent." New York *Morning Chronicle*, 1802–3 (reprinted, New York: William H. Clayton, 1824).

Salmagundi; or, The Whim-Whams and Opinions of Launcelot Langstaff, Esq., and Others. New York: David Longworth, 1807–8.

A History of New York, from the Beginning of the World to the End of the Dutch Dynasty. New York: Inskeep and Bradford, 1809.

The Sketch Book of Geoffrey Crayon, Gent. New York: C. S. Van Winkle, 1819–20; London: John Miller, 1820.

Bracebridge Hall, or, The Humorists. A Medley. New York: C. S. Van Winkle, 1822; London: John Murray, 1822.

Tales of a Traveller. Philadelphia: H. C. Carey and I. Lea, 1824; London: John Murray, 1824.

A History of the Life and Voyages of Christopher Columbus. New York: G. and C. Carvill, 1828; London: John Murray, 1828.

Chronicle of the Conquest of Granada. Philadelphia: Carey, Lea, and Carey, 1829; London: John Murray, 1829.

Voyages and Discoveries of the Companions of Columbus. Philadelphia: Carey and Lea, 1831; London: John Murray, 1831.

The Alhambra. Philadelphia: Carey and Lea, 1832; London: Henry Colburn and Richard Bentley, 1832.

The Crayon Miscellany. Philadelphia: Carey and Lea, 1835. As *Miscellanies*, London: John Murray, 1835. (*A Tour on the Prairies*, separately published, London: John Murray, 1835; Paris: Galignani, 1835.)

Astoria, or, Anecdotes of an Enterprise beyond the Rocky Mountains. Philadelphia: Carey, Lea and Blanchard, 1836.

The Rocky Mountains: or, Scenes, Incidents, and Adventures in the Far West;

Digested from the Journal of Captain B. L. E. Bonneville, of the Army of the United States, and Illustrated from Various Other Sources. Philadelphia: Lea and Blanchard, 1837. As *Adventures of Captain Bonneville*, London: Richard Bentley, 1837; Paris: Galignani, 1837.

Oliver Goldsmith: A Biography. New York: G. P. Putnam, 1849.

A Book of the Hudson. New York: G. P. Putnam, 1849.

Mahomet and His Successors. New York: G. P. Putnam, 1850.

Wolfert's Roost. New York. G. P. Putnam, 1855.

Life of George Washington. New York: G. P. Putnam, 1855–59.

Spanish Papers and Other Miscellanies. New York: G. P. Putnam, 1866.

The Wild Huntsman. Boston: Bibliophile Society, 1924.

Abu Hassan. Boston: Bibliophile Society, 1924.

Journals

Journal of Washington Irving, 1803, edited by Stanley T. Williams. New York: Oxford University Press, 1934.

Washington Irving: Notes and Journal of Travel in Europe, 1804–1805, edited by William P. Trent. 3 vols. New York: Grolier Club, 1921.

"Washington Irving's Notebook of 1810," edited by Barbara D. Simison, *Yale University Library Gazette,* 24:1–16, 74–94 (Winter, Spring 1949).

The Journals of Washington Irving [1815–42], edited by William P. Trent and George S. Hellman. 3 vols. Boston: Bibliophile Society, 1919.

Tour in Scotland, 1817, and Other Manuscript Notes, edited by Stanley T. Williams. New Haven: Yale University Press, 1927.

Washington Irving: Notes While Preparing a Sketch Book, &c 1817, edited by Stanley T. Williams. New Haven: Yale University Press, 1927.

Journal of Washington Irving (1823–1824), edited by Stanley T. Williams. Cambridge, Mass.: Harvard University Press, 1931.

"Washington Irving's Madrid Journal, 1827–1828," edited by Andrew B. Myers, *Bulletin of the New York Public Library,* 62:217–27, 300–11, 407–19, 463–71 (1958).

Washington Irving Diary, Spain, 1828–1829, edited by Clara Louisa Penney. New York: Hispanic Society of America, 1930.

The Western Journals of Washington Irving, edited by John Francis Mc-Dermott. Norman: University of Oklahoma Press, 1944.

Current American Reprints

Astoria. New York: Dolphin. $1.45. 2 vols. Philadelphia: Keystone. $1.95 each.

The Legend of Sleepy Hollow and Other Selections from Washington Irving. New York: Washington Square Press. $.60.

Selected Prose. New York: Holt, Rinehart, and Winston. $1.25.
The Sketch Book. New York: Dolphin. $.95. New York: New American Library.
   $.60.

Biographies

Bowers, Claude G. *The Spanish Adventures of Washington Irving*. Boston:
   Houghton Mifflin, 1940.
Cater, Harold Dean. *Washington Irving at Sunnyside*. Tarrytown: Sleepy Hol-
   low Restorations, 1957.
Hellman, George S. *Washington Irving Esquire, Ambassador at Large from the
   New World to the Old*. New York: Knopf, 1925.
Irving, Pierre M. *The Life and Letters of Washington Irving*. 4 vols. New
   York: G. P. Putnam, 1862–64.
Pochmann, Henry A., ed. *Washington Irving: Representative Selections*. New
   York: American Book, 1934.
Reichart, Walter A. *Washington Irving and Germany*. Ann Arbor: University
   of Michigan Press, 1957.
Wagenknecht, Edward. *Washington Irving: Moderation Displayed*. New York:
   Oxford University Press, 1962.
Williams, Stanley T. *The Life of Washington Irving*. 2 vols. New York: Oxford
   University Press, 1935.

Criticism

Beach, Leonard. "Washington Irving: The Artist in a Changing World," *Uni-
   versity of Kansas City Review*, 14:259–66 (Summer 1948).
Brooks, Van Wyck. *The World of Washington Irving*. New York: Doubleday,
   1944.
Hedges, William L. "Irving's *Columbus*: The Problem of Romantic Biog-
   raphy," *The Americas*, 13:127–40 (1956).
Hoffman, Daniel G. "Irving's Use of American Folklore in 'The Legend of
   Sleepy Hollow,' " *PMLA*, 68:425–35 (June 1953).
Hoffman, Louise M. "Irving's Use of Spanish Sources in *The Conquest of
   Granada*," *Hispania*, 28:483–98 (November 1945).
Laird, C. G. "Tragedy and Irony in *Knickerbocker's History*," *American Litera-
   ture*, 12:157–72 (May 1940).
LeFevre, Louis. "Paul Bunyan and Rip Van Winkle," *Yale Review*, 36:66–76
   (Autumn 1946).
Leisy, E. E. "Irving and the Genteel Tradition," *Sewanee Review*, 21:223–27
   (September 1946).
Lloyd, F. V. "Irving's *Rip Van Winkle*," *Explicator*, 4:26 (February 1946).

47

Martin, Terrence. "Rip, Ichabod, and the American Imagination," *American Literature*, 31:137–49 (May 1959).

Pochmann, Henry A. "Irving's German Sources in *The Sketch Book*," *Studies in Philology*, 27:477–507 (July 1930).

Snell, George. "Washington Irving: A Revaluation," *Modern Language Quarterly*, 7:303–10 (September 1946).

Webster, C. M. "Irving's Expurgation of the 1809 *A History of New York*," *American Literature*, 4:293–95 (November 1932).

Wegelin, Christopher. "Dickens and Irving: The Problem of Influence," *Modern Language Quarterly*, 7:83–91 (November 1932).

Young, Philip. "Fallen from Time: The Mythic Rip Van Winkle," *Kenyon Review*, 22:547–73 (Autumn 1960).

DATE DUE